C 1996   7/96

The Children of
BOLIVIA

THE WORLD'S CHILDREN

The Children of
BOLIVIA

JULES HERMES

Carolrhoda Books, Inc./Minneapolis

*For Jean Marie and Rehana Lafont. Your kindness
will always be remembered.*

*Special thanks to Tim and Colleen Stellmach, Tim Stellmach Jr.,
Darius Morgan, the Madres Franciscanas in Coroico and Carmen
Pampa, and Teresa Glass.*

*The publisher wishes to thank Connie Weil, Professor of Geography
at the University of Minnesota, for her valuable assistance in the
preparation of this book.*

Carolrhoda Books, Inc. c/o The Lerner Group
241 First Avenue North, Minneapolis, MN 55401

LIBRARY OF CONGRESS CATALOGING-IN-PUBLICATION DATA

Hermes, Jules, 1962–
    The children of Bolivia / Jules Hermes.
      p. cm. — (The world's children)
    Includes index.
    ISBN 0-87614-935-2
    1. Bolivia—Social life and customs—Juvenile literature. 2. Children—Bolivia—
Social life and customs—Juvenile literature. [1. Bolivia—Social life and customs.]
I. Title. II. Series: World's children (Minneapolis, Minn.)
F3310.H47   1996
984—dc20   94-44092
                                                                          CIP
                                                                          AC

Manufactured in the United States of America

1 2 3 4 5 6 – JR – 01 00 99 98 97 96

Author's Note

Flying into La Paz, Bolivia, was a spectacular experience. From the window of the plane, I caught my first sight of the snowcapped Andes Mountains and of Mount Illimani, which stands over La Paz at 21,000 feet above sea level. Bolivia held many "firsts" for me: my first river trip into the Amazon Basin; my first sight of a sloth, a spider monkey, and an alpaca; and my first visit inside a working mine. Because of Bolivia's incredibly rugged terrain, it was the first time I found travel difficult, sometimes not possible at all.

It was the people of this landlocked, isolated country that especially held my attention. Proud and determined, the people of Bolivia hold on to their distinct languages and ways of life that have outlasted the groups that have come to conquer them. They teach their children that they must keep their culture alive. Bolivians pass the age-old secrets of their ancestors on to their children, who hold them in their hearts and minds with a power as great as the stars in the night sky.

Bolivia is a land of amazing diversity. A traveler can go from the snowy peaks of the Andes Mountains in the west to steamy rain forests in the north, and then find low, open grasslands in the east. Situated in the heart of South America, Bolivia covers an area about twice the size of Texas.

The Andes Mountains spread into two major ranges in Bolivia. Between them lies the Altiplano, or high plateau, which holds about half the country's eight million people. This vast, desolate region once cradled an ancient civilization known as Tiahuanaco, which reached its peak around A.D. 900. In the 1400s and 1500s, the Altiplano became part of the great Inca Empire. Then in 1532, Spanish

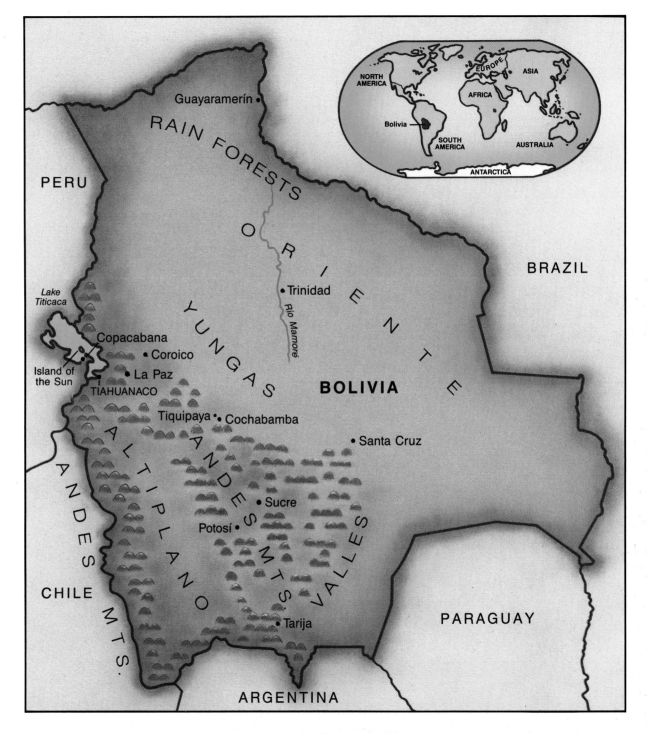

conquistadores, or conquerors, arrived in Bolivia and defeated the Incas. Spain ruled Bolivia until 1825.

Two main groups of native peoples account for about 60 percent of Bolivia's population. One group, the Aymara, are probably descendants of the Tiahuanacans. The other group, the Quechua, are descended from the Incas. In Bolivia, native people are called *campesinos,* which means "country people." *Mestizos*—people of mixed Spanish and native ancestry—make up about 30 percent of the population. The remaining 10 percent are people of European heritage. Most of them are descended from Spanish colonists.

María lives along the shores of Lake Titicaca. Like an inland sea, Lake Titicaca covers 3,200 square miles and has dozens of tiny islands scattered throughout its waters. María and her family live on the Island of the Sun, the largest and most sacred of these islands. The 300 Aymara who live in María's *comunidad* (community or village) get most of their food by fishing the icy waters of Lake Titicaca.

María's *comunidad* carries on traditions from long ago. Boys learn to make boats from totora reeds found along the shores of Lake Titicaca. Girls learn to weave the wool of alpacas and llamas into beautiful blankets and sweaters.

Using llamas and alpacas to carry their goods, María and her family travel by foot on the island. María takes care of her own alpaca. She says alpacas can be very naughty. When one is angry, it will spit or try to bite people.

Right: *María with her alpaca. In western Bolivia, alpacas and llamas serve as pack animals and also provide wool and meat. Below: María's mother weaves the wool of an alpaca into a blanket for her family.*

Opposite page: *The Andes Mountains loom beyond Lake Titicaca, the highest navigable lake in the world. Aymara fish for trout and bass in the freezing waters of the lake.*

María attends a small village school, but much of what she learns comes from legends handed down by her ancestors. She especially likes the stories of the Incas. One legend says that when they were trying to stop the invading Spaniards from finding their treasure, the Incas cast their gold and jewels into the middle of Lake Titicaca. Some people say that piles of riches still lie on the bottom of the lake.

The farthest María has been from her home is the town of Copacabana on the south shore of Lake Titicaca. During the 1400s, Copacabana was a rest stop for Inca travelers on their way to the *huaca*—a sacred place on the Island of the Sun. Bolivians now journey to Copacabana to visit a special statue. Known as the Virgin of Copacabana, the statue was carved in honor of the Virgin Mary, who some people believe appeared in Copacabana in 1582.

Bolivians often bring their new cars to this church, which houses the Virgin of Copacabana. They decorate the cars with fresh flowers; then a priest sprinkles holy water under the hood and says a blessing.

María's *comunidad* celebrates the end of the school year. Aymaran celebrations usually involve dancing, loud music, and firecrackers that can be heard all day and night.

East of Lake Titicaca, the Altiplano suddenly drops into a 1,000-foot-deep basin. Sprawling in this basin is La Paz—Bolivia's largest city and one of its two capitals. Life in La Paz seems to be layered. *Campesinos* live at higher altitudes near the rim. Wealthy people live more comfortably at the city's lower altitudes.

Grover lives in the upper part of La Paz, in a small house with no telephone or television. After school, he often rides a *micro,* a small public bus, down a spiraling road to the suburb of La Florida. Grover's father works at a large mansion there as a gardener, handyman, and cook. Grover sometimes gets to watch television or play a video game at the mansion. Usually, though, he helps his father in the garden or the kitchen.

La Paz is the highest capital city in the world.

Grover

Aymara campesinas *line up along El Prado, part of La Paz's main avenue, during a march through the city. They wear typical Aymaran clothing—a shawl, a full skirt called a* pollera, *and a bowler hat.*

13

Occasionally, the streets of La Paz overflow with thousands of Aymara demonstrating for higher wages and workers' rights. Traffic comes to a halt, firecrackers burst in the air, and the determined Aymara demand to be heard.

Grover and his father

Campesinos in La Paz make an average wage of 200 bolivianos (about 50 dollars) per month. (The boliviano is the basic unit of money in Bolivia.) Grover feels lucky that his father works for a family that pays him more than the average. Many of his friends, he says, are not so fortunate.

A social revolution in 1952 brought about great improvements in the lives of Bolivia's *campesinos.* For the first time, all adult Bolivians were allowed to vote. Some of the land that had been taken by the Spaniards was returned to *campesinos.* Since the revolution, however, frequent changes in government leadership have taken away many of the reforms. Bolivian *campesinos* still struggle to keep their rights and to improve their standard of living.

Plaza Murillo, in the heart of La Paz, is named for Pedro Domingo Murillo, who helped Bolivians gain independence from Spain. The plaza is a popular gathering spot for people of all ages.

While La Paz is Bolivia's actual capital, the city of Sucre is its official capital. Nine-year-old Weimar Alata lives in Sucre and attends the Escuela Mixta school. Weimar is considered a *mestizo:* his mother is mostly Spanish and his father is Quechuan. He and his family participate in traditional Quechuan fiestas, or popular festivals and carnivals. But they also wear modern, European clothes and have adopted modern ways of life. In school, Weimar usually speaks Spanish, and at home he speaks his father's language, Quechua. Weimar takes his studies quite seriously and hopes his education will someday reward him with a good job.

Founded by the Spaniards in 1538, Sucre has glorious churches and Spanish colonial architecture. By city law, most buildings must be kept whitewashed, as they have been for centuries.

Above: *Weimar* (top row, center) *plays with his friends before school begins.*

Opposite page: *The red-tiled roofs and whitewashed churches of Sucre reveal the influence of Spanish architecture in Bolivia.* Opposite page, inset: *Statues of Roman Catholic saints adorn this clock tower, which sits atop a hospital in Sucre.*

Right: *Before going to school or work in Sucre, people stop to buy hot tea.*

A Bolivian market is as much a social gathering as it is a place to do business.

The southern peaks of the Andes drop off gradually into sloping hills and wide fertile valleys. Known as the Valles, this area is the heart of Bolivian agriculture. Most Quechua in Bolivia live on the southern rim of the Altiplano and in the Valles.

Rosa lives in Cliza, a town situated in a lush valley. Cliza is home to nearly 5,000 Quechua, who live mostly from farming and raising animals. Well-known for its Sunday market, Cliza attracts hundreds of villagers from the region, who come to buy and sell produce, animals, and clothing. Rosa and her mother sell chickens and potatoes that they raise on their small patch of land. Potatoes were first raised in the Andes Mountains and were unknown to the rest of the world until the Spaniards brought them to Europe.

Above: *Rosa and her mother.*
Left: *The Cliza market. In contrast
to the Aymaran bowler hat and
full* pollera *skirt, Quechua women
often wear a stovepipe hat and a
shorter, pleated skirt.*

Left: *Elisabeth.* Below: *Elisabeth leads younger girls through the streets of Tiquipaya during the Festival of St. Michael.*

Elisabeth lives in Tiquipaya, another Quechua town in the Valles. Once a year, all of Tiquipaya celebrates the Festival of St. Michael—the feast day of the town's patron saint. Nearly every town in Bolivia has a patron saint, and every saint has a feast day. During fiesta time, the sleepy town of Tiquipaya comes alive and bursts with color.

For several months beforehand, Elisabeth practices the dance she and her friends will perform. Her mother works hard sewing Elisabeth's fancy costume. Elisabeth and her friends enjoy fiestas and consider it an honor to participate, though it is expensive. Elisabeth says it is their obligation to their town and their families to carry on their traditions.

Hundreds of young people perform dances during the festival.

Juan Carlos also lives in Tiquipaya. Since he was four years old, Juan Carlos has been dancing the Tinku—a dance that represents the Incas' fight against the Spanish *conquistadores*. Dances are very important in Bolivian culture. Some dances, such as the Tinku, tell a story. Others celebrate an event such as a wedding.

Like Juan Carlos, most Bolivians follow the Roman Catholic faith. Most Bolivians also observe some ancient Quechua or Aymara religious beliefs and traditions. Combining the old and the new, Bolivian fiestas often begin with a grand religious procession that honors a Catholic saint. Much of the music and dance that follows dates back to the time of the Incas or before.

The boys of Tiquipaya dance the Tinku at the Festival of St. Michael.

Opposite page: *After five hours of dancing, Juan Carlos and his friends take a break.* Right: *Juan Carlos.* Far right: *The masked* Diablada, *or devil dancers, appear in many fiestas throughout Bolivia.*

Hernán and Alberto live in Tarija, a region of Bolivia that shares a border with Argentina. Tarijans tend to have more in common with their Argentinean neighbors than with other Bolivians. Many Tarijans also resemble Argentineans, most of whom have Spanish or Italian ancestry.

A Quechua woman prunes grapevines in Tarija, the only grape-growing region in Bolivia.

Hernán and Alberto shine shoes in the city of Tarija's main plaza. A few blocks away, Hernán's mother sells exotic flowers at the city market. Hernán and Alberto say that Tarija's dry, sunny weather is the best in all of Bolivia. The markets of Tarija offer a variety of produce—such as grapes, peaches, and oranges—not often available in the rest of Bolivia.

Right: *Hernán and Alberto.* Below left: *Hernán's mother* (left) *sells flowers.* Below right: *Tarija markets offer an appealing variety of fruits.*

Before the Spanish *conquista-dores* arrived in Bolivia in 1532, the Inca Empire was a prosperous farming society. When silver and other minerals were discovered at Cerro Rico—Rich Mountain—above the town of Potosí, the Spaniards seized the Incas' lands. They forced the Incas and other native Bolivians to work in mines under brutal conditions. Spanish settlers became very rich from the precious minerals.

By the 1880s, most of Bolivia's silver deposits had been exhausted, and the country turned to mining tin. But during the 1980s, the world tin market collapsed, leaving 80 percent of Bolivia's miners without jobs.

Smaller mining operations continue. Twelve-year-old Sumayla lives with her family at the mouth of the Rosario silver mine, located in Cerro Rico. Mining has been a part of her family's life for generations.

Sumayla stands at the front door of her home in Potosí.

Right: *For up to 10 hours a day, Sumayla's father works in tiny chambers inside the Rosario mine.*
Below: *Cerro Rico towers over the mining town of Potosí. It has been calculated that the silver taken from Cerro Rico could form a bridge from Bolivia to Spain.*

Conditions and methods of mining remain much as they were 200 years ago. Temperatures vary greatly in the mines from extreme heat to damp cold. Miners use dynamite to blast farther into the earth, and tunnels sometimes collapse without warning. To cope with these conditions, miners chew leaves of the coca plant, which help the body handle cold, hunger, and fatigue. Coca-chewing is as common among Bolivian *campesinos* as coffee-drinking is among workers in the United States.

Sumayla worries about her father's health and safety. Every morning, she makes a lunch for her father to take into the mine. Then she says a special prayer and makes an offering of tea to the Pachamama, or Mother Earth. She asks the Pachamama to keep her father and the other miners safe.

Women sell dynamite to miners in the Potosí market.

Miners pack their cheeks with coca leaves, replenishing their supply throughout the long day.

Sumayla helps her father carry his equipment to the mouth of the Rosario silver mine.

Under Spanish rule, thousands of native Bolivians died from working in the mines and from diseases brought by the Spaniards. Searching for more laborers, the Spaniards turned to the continent of Africa. Africans were brought over on crowded ships and forced to work in the mines. Unable to adapt to the cooler climate and high altitude, Africans died even more quickly than did the native Bolivians. Those who survived left Potosí and settled in the Yungas, the jungle valleys east of the northern Andes.

Esmerajilda lives in Mururata, one of two villages in the Yungas inhabited by descendants of African mine workers. She lives much like the Aymara of the region. She dresses Aymaran, and she works on her family's small plot of land. The Aymara have absorbed African dances and drumming into their fiestas. Esmerajilda says the best time to see the mixture of cultures is at fiesta time in nearby Coroico.

Esmerajilda

Above: *Esmerajilda wears a traditional Aymaran festival costume.*
Left: *Coroico*

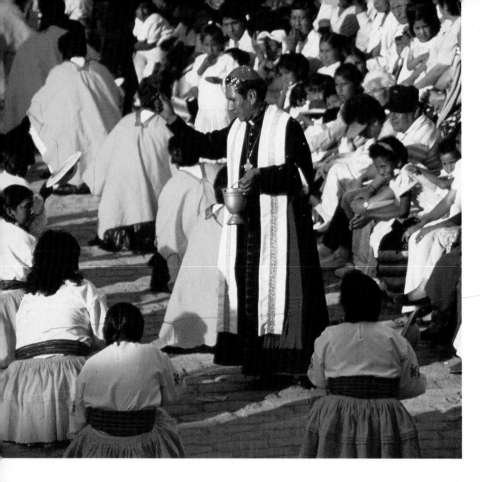

Every year, Esmerajilda and other villagers travel by bus or by foot to Coroico for the Festival of the Virgin of Candelaría. Dozens of other groups from all over also come to celebrate. The fiesta begins with a magnificent procession, as the statue of the Virgin Mary is carried around the town plaza, followed by dancers and bands.

The villagers of Mururata perform special dances in memory of the hardships of their ancestors. Pedro comes from Mururata and performs a dance called the Morenada. Morenada costumes make fun of the court dress of the Spanish *conquistadores*. Slow, pounding drums accompany the dancers, who slash and whip the main dancer as he crawls on the ground in chains. No one sleeps much during fiesta week, as blasting bands play music throughout the night.

Above left: *Dancers receive a blessing from the Catholic bishop on the first day of the Festival of the Virgin of Candelaría. On the last night, everyone gathers in the church for midnight mass.* Above: *Pedro dances the Morenada.*

Festival-goers parade the statue of the Virgin Mary around the town plaza.

Angelina has come from La Paz to dance in the Festival of the Virgin of Candelaría. Bolivians of all ages, classes, and ethnic groups celebrate together.

33

Because the people of the Yungas are spread out over rugged terrain, few schools exist for children of the region. Isabel and Basilia attend San Francisco Xavier school in Carmen Pampa, located one hour outside Coroico. Like most of their classmates, they must walk about two hours along jungle trails to reach the school.

Most of the children who attend San Francisco Xavier live and work on their families' coca farms. Coca bushes grow in abundance throughout the Yungas and other valleys farther south. The leaves of the plant are sold legally in Bolivian markets. Whether chewed or made into tea, coca leaves act as a mild stimulant, much like the caffeine in coffee.

However, much of Bolivia's coca crop is refined into the dangerous, illegal drug cocaine and then sold in other countries. The U.S. government has offered to pay Bolivian farmers to switch to other crops. The farmers have resisted, however, because they can earn far more money from coca than from any other crop. Experts say that coca accounts for at least as much income as do all of Bolivia's legal exports.

Above: *A truck slowly winds its way along a difficult road in the Yungas.* Opposite page: *Students at San Francisco Xavier take their morning milk break* (top). *Isabel and Basilia* (bottom)

Many of Bolivia's farmers grow coca, the plant used to make the illegal drug cocaine.

A single road curls its way along a narrow cliff from the Yungas to El Beni—one of the most unexplored parts of South America's Amazon Basin. The jungle becomes so thick in many parts of this region that people can travel only by boat. The area's rivers once served as highways for boats transporting products such as rubber, mahogany wood, cashews, and Brazil nuts. Roads have mostly replaced rivers as the main highways, but rivers are still used by smaller transport operations or when roads are flooded.

Dublio knows this region well. He comes from the jungle town of Guayaramerín, located on one of Bolivia's longest rivers, the Río Mamoré. Dublio and his father make their living delivering goods up and down the river on a cargo boat called the *Yuventus*. They travel for days, sometimes weeks, depending on the weather.

With a cargo of bananas, wood, and gasoline, the Yuventus *and its crew depart from the banks of the Río Mamoré. Dublio, in the red hat, is the youngest crew member.*

Opposite page: *Sunset on the Río Mamoré*

The destination of the *Yuventus* is usually Trinidad, the largest town in El Beni. The journey can get boring, says Dublio, whose main job is loading and unloading cargo. But once in a while something exciting happens. Sometimes the *Yuventus* picks up villagers who have a small load to take up the Río Mamoré. On one trip, Dublio and the crew helped a woman and her daughter, Loraina, whose boat was caught in a whirlpool on the river. One of the crewmen jumped into the water, swam to the woman, and helped her row the boat upstream to the waiting *Yuventus*. Dublio helped them unload their cargo of bananas, coconuts, and sacks of rice onto the *Yuventus* for safety. Then the *Yuventus* towed the smaller boat to a place where the river's current was less dangerous.

A crewman helps Loraina and her mother out of a whirlpool in the river.

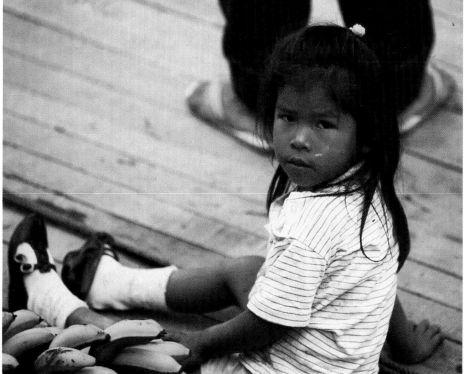

Dublio ties the smaller boat to the Yuventus.

Loraina waits while Dublio finishes unloading her mother's cargo.

Fabiola and her monkey, Antonia, live in Baranca Colorado, a tiny comunidad *in the jungle. The only way to reach Baranca Colorado is by boat.*

Dublio and the crew often stop at a *comunidad* along the Río Mamoré to visit friends or to join in a fiesta. Today, the *Yuventus* stops at Baranca Colorado for the celebration of All Souls' Day. Both Catholic and *campesino* traditions place great importance on the souls of the dead. Many Bolivians believe their ancestors guide them through life and watch over them.

Dublio and the rest of the crew join a family in Baranca Colorado for a light meal of fish cooked in coconut milk. Later, they walk through the jungle to the cemetery, where they say prayers and make offerings of drinks and gifts to the ancestors of Baranca Colorado.

Villagers gather at the cemetery in Baranca Colorado to pray for their ancestors on All Souls' Day.

Crocodiles populate the Río Mamoré and other rivers of northeastern Bolivia.

41

María and Madeline

Fast-food restaurants, electronics stores, and posh clothing shops line the streets of Santa Cruz.

Sloths are native to the area around Santa Cruz and sometimes appear in the city. A very slow mover, the sloth can live its entire life in one tree.

Rivers and narrow waterways were once the only way to travel in the Oriente—Bolivia's vast eastern lowlands. Few people lived in the resource-rich region, and trade was difficult. But in the 1950s, the government built a road connecting Santa Cruz, the Oriente's major city, with La Paz. Workers came to drill newly discovered oil deposits, and new farmlands were opened up. Santa Cruz ballooned to a population of nearly one million people by 1990, making it Bolivia's second largest city.

María and Madeline moved to Santa Cruz when they were babies, after their father began working at an oil refinery. The girls attend a Catholic school in Santa Cruz. After school, they like going to the city center with their mother to buy fresh food for the evening meal. They also enjoy looking at clothes and records in the city shopping centers.

The people of Bolivia have overcome many obstacles. Since gaining independence from Spain, Bolivians have had unending problems building a stable economy and government. Bolivia lost more than half its territory in wars with its neighbors. Despite the discovery of oil and natural gas deposits and improvements in transportation, Bolivia remains South America's poorest country.

Nevertheless, the *campesinos* of Bolivia have survived with a kind of pride no conquerors or wars can ever destroy. Bolivians of all ages and ethnic groups work together to develop new industries and to improve their country. They continue to celebrate with great zest their love for life and for each other.

Pronunciation Guide

Altiplano ahl-tee-PLAH-noh
Andes AN-deez
Aymara eye-mah-RAH
campesinos kahm-pay-SEE-nohs
comunidad koh-moo-nee-DAHD
Guayaramerín gwy-ah-rah-meh-REEN
huaca oo-AH-kah
mestizo meh-STEE-zoh
micro MEE-kroh
Potosí poh-toh-SEE
Quechua KETCH-wah
Río Mamoré REE-oh mah-moh-RAY
Sucre SOO-kray
Tarija tah-REE-hah
Tiahuanaco tee-ah-wah-NAH-koh
Tiquipaya tee-kee-PAH-yuh
Titicaca tih-tih-KAH-kah
Valles VAH-yays

Index